Poems of Trials, Triumphs, and Turtles

Poems of Trials, Triumphs, and Turtles
By Sandy Lender

Sandy Lender Ink's IYF Publishing
Dragon Hoard Press/Florida

Sandy Lender Ink Inc.
Florida
USA

Originally published in the United States of America.

ISBN 978-1-7345152-2-0

Printed in the United States of America

Book design by Sandy Lender

Dedication
As always,
for my Petri,
who now rests
at the center of the universe

And for Josh, the water turtle, too

Table of Contents

Introduction

While my creative writing strength lies in novels, I've dabbled in poetry for a few decades. It's a joy to use poetry for characters' inner musings, and to practice thoughts and emotions for scenes through verse. A sampling of my rhyming and non-rhyming mental exercises felt edited—and re-edited—enough to share with the world. But I needed to separate this sampling of verses into sections for sense and clarity.

Part I of this book includes only four poems I wrote for the dear and darling pets in my life. (Because releasing in December 2019 an entire book titled "How to Train Your Human: A Guide for Parrots" with, for, and by my parrot Petri wasn't an indulgent enough tribute.)

Part II explores a time in history that tested our collective mettle. Once I returned from a nine-day convention and tradeshow in mid-March 2020, too many people in North America were losing their minds over paper products. As ridiculous as that shortage became, people experienced everything from fear to lost wages to anxiety to domestic violence to bullying from anyone who considered them selfish for needing to get out of exile to feed their families. A few of the poems in Part II address that period of time, but I didn't want to dwell on that point in history. Instead, Part II shares a touch of cynicism, a bit of fun, and a ray of hope before we dive into the general life section of Part III.

A handful of American Realism poems nestle among the more hopeful and uplifting lines in this portion of the book. Part III delves into the emotions and colors we feel and see when deep, realistic truths give way to good, glorious hopes. Again, I tried to keep the sorrowful side of reality to a minimum; we have so much to look forward to in the friendships and faith of this life.

All my best to you,
Sandy Lender

Part I
Pet Poetry

Gimme Your Smile

Gimme your smile
Gimme your song
A tune to go with me
All my day long

Let dawn's sunrise
Brighten your eye
Let your cute countenance
Fill up my sky

Carry the sunshine
Every day
Shatter the storm clouds
Wherever you play

Cast a rainbow
Into the trees
Spotlight the songbirds
Amid canopies

Gimme your laugh
Gimme your smile
Something to last
A goodly long while

For wherever you are
Your light, too, will be
Lightening life
Enough to soothe me

Love on the Rocks

Green eyes sparkle heavenward
A look of sheer amazement
Dare I say love?
I've never seen a turtle look
At a human with adoration
She stares,
Gazing. Waiting.
For my hand to drop food into the water
    Plop!
    Splash!
    Dart and dash!
She's nomming down each piece
...as if I hadn't just fed her this morning

I wish I could do better
Give her fancier food more often
A better filter
More time in the pond I built out back
Stronger lights over a range
Of bigger basking areas
For completely drying
Destroying ickies on her shell

After she consumes all the pieces
All the noms scarfed down
Into her sizeable belly
She climbs back onto the rocks
And stretches her neck up
Toward me
Her green eyes sparkling again
As if asking me to turn up
The Neil Diamond 8-Track in the background
For her basking pleasure this afternoon

Slow Dancing, Swaying to the Music

A familiar melody caught me off guard today.
I'd forgotten singing this one to you
Forgotten the first time ever I saw your face
More than the memory of you swaying...
More than remembering you
        closing your eyes to soak in the ambiance
        of being fully, completely, lovingly adored
More than the vision of you content
I sense a peaceful, easy feeling
        as if you're near enough to hear
        this unchained melody with me again

One Conure to Rule Them All

THIS JUST IN: Scientists confirm
      at the center of the universe
      in his most resplendent yellow and orange
      with hints of royal and sapphire blue
      on his green tail feathers

      TOWERS MY PET PARROT.

or...
  rather...
    He sometimes leans,
resting comfortably against his cozy hut,
one foot tucked serenely to his ample belly
while he alternately snoozes
or watches The History Channel,
collecting ideas
to rule the universe around him.

Part II
March 15 – April 30, 2020

Panic at the Corner Store

The number of trees sacrificed
for our hygienic needs recently skyrocketed
to refuel our sudden gluttony
      in this time of insanity
But I hear the pipeline's restocking itself while I lament the death of
my wine Houdini

I consider
(Only briefly)
How fortunate
How privileged
The grid still functions
Spewing cool air
To cool feverish hallucinations
Brought on by cooled stock-market climbs
...
And bearish misgivings
Of corkscrew-twisting anxiety into some semblance of relief

Video from space shows pollution has cleared over China
At least...
It's cleared over the areas where the crematoriums aren't
      pumping ash like the Nazi death camps of old.

But, hey, the trees can't be slaughtered if no one's reporting for
duty
      in this time of insanity

Florida Update

As a Floridian,
I'm used to
updates every four hours.
I know how to read cones of uncertainty
and noodles
plotting the probability of my demise.

It turns out the end of the world has more frequent updates.

Between them
I set YouTube to autoplay
Anticipating Janet Armstrong's voice
will absolutely harmonize with Bowie
Alongside a sax solo
While the reports of the dead toll in on the TV screen.

Morbid?
Yes.
But...
Like my friends popping Clonazepam on the reg,
Texting our shared angst,
I'm transfixed by this constant need for numbers

Percentages

How many of my neighbors currently walking their teacup-size
chihuahuas will succumb
What time will Publix open for those of us under the age of 65
Is CVS allowing pickup of maintenance medications in the drive-thru

I'm paralyzed

I hallucinate superheroes deliver Four Roses
40 proof to settle anxiety caused by the too-measured brunette the
red-and-gray corona-graphic reveals on the TV screen

Once an hour seems hardly enough
To feed our need for cone-less information

I absolutely ask you
For whom the bell tolls
At the next update

Pity Party

It's mentally exhausting to work ten-hour days
six days a week
while so many are home talking about creativity.
Like a fool,
I mentioned this to a friend.
"You're lucky to still have a job," he told me.
And I have to agree.

It's my own fault that I can't partake of the handout
everyone else is receiving.
"You should have filed differently last year," my friend told me.
And I know he's right.

I pay eight hundred dollars a month for my health insurance
premium
and feel a bit rude complaining about that because,
to be fair,
I'm lucky Blue Cross didn't drop me eight years ago.
No one survives cancer without financial punishment.
"You should be thankful you have insurance," my friend told me.
And I have to agree.

My car insurance company isn't giving me a break
for leaving my car parked during stay-at-home orders.
My mortgage company isn't giving me a pass
on this month's house payment.
The electric company isn't letting me
put off paying my bill until June or July
like everybody else gets to do...
"You're lucky to have a car," my friend reminded me.
"You're lucky to have a house," my friend told me.
"You're lucky to have electricity," my friend said.
And he's absolutely right.

It's all in one's attitude—this life.
I am thankful.
I am grateful.
I know I've climbed tall cliffs to have a job that pays the bills
through even a nerve-wracking pandemic.
So I shut. my. mouth.
Keep my worries inside
Push my feelings of being slighted down deep
Down deep in that pit where survivors put all their guilt
In the pit where all my friend's factually correct statements live

White Gold Haiku

Taken for granted
Plied with softest promises
Dryness denied me

Bringing the Top Down

gnashing teeth of angry crowds
impatient hordes
with rams and torches
crowding for a promised handout
they've chased their champion
      to the top floor
of the stronghold he's still building
banging maces at its braces
its unfinished foundations
as they lean into the stoning
and slide off sides of blood pooling
all the while pointing
fists and swords to the top floor
which splinters under the weight
      of a world's condemnation

40 Days

After 40 days of random sorrow
Having killed one tiny spider for each day
     of isolation
My spirit feels broken by multitudes of clouds gathered
Thank God they finally burst
     heaviness emptied on our world
     to wash down pollen-coated signs
     and posts
     and hosts of worries cleansed

After 40 days of intolerable waiting
Your text message set a rainbow in my sky
Like a million tiny spiders floating on their parachute webs
     away into a sunny horizon
Carrying whispered melodies
     to lift up spirits
          stepping out to light
          and stare at speckles drifting by

Breath Returning

Glass sandpaper scours the planet's forest lungs
Scrubbing free the smog once stuck to skyscrapers
So that it breaks
Rises
Floats away
Beyond the atmosphere
Burning upon out-ry

A mere foot above sea level
Worms dangling from over-green branches
Shudder in their shells
Until splendor erupts
In oranges and golds not witnessed for decades.
A century of smoke
And progress dissipated
Under the whisper of wispy wings

Butterflies lift to the skies
And pollens release in puffs of spores
And scores of seeds
Restored
Amid the buzz of bees
And my soft breath sounds
In my own quiet space
Interrupted only when I hum along
With a bird's twittered song
I swear I recognize from my infancy
When my lungs were as clean as the forests now returning

Part III
Bits of Life and Living Upward

Anti-Rust

External woes succumb
to daydreams
of patent-pending miracles
on the shortest medicine cabinet shelf
where the expensive vials sit.
They promise timelessness,
the smooth perfection
of Bowie, 1971,
asking if there's life on Mars.
A promise I'll get that fancy feeling
from someone at the reunion saying,
"You haven't aged a day."
As if these strangers have the right
to randomly validate me,
ask what cream I use
for my silver screen appearance,
when my internal soundtrack
of personal affirmation
is my patent-pending secret
and all the validation
against corrosion I need.

Don't Diss the Carpet

My buyer's agent called it "shag carpet" derisively,
after I'd trekked three hours to see the home.

Home.

I had, in my younger years, seen actual shag carpet;
this didn't fit that description.
This offered fullness and warmth for one's feet.
Its marbled brown and tan would hide dirt,
all manner of accidents,
and past sins.
Its padding offered comfort.
There was a consistency about it throughout the modest home.

Home.

It did *not* have the tall, straw-like blend of shag
from the God-awful '70s.
I smiled politely, before checking light switches,
faucets,
commode,
closet door tracks,
while he took an important call from a client.

Left alone with my thoughts,
I stepped out of my flip-flops
so my toes could knead the fibers
while I stared out a sun-filled portal.
Yes, comforting.
I would get two windows in the room I chose for sleep
and two in the room I chose for my library in this...

if this...

Interrupting my interior decorating,
the lad asked if I was ready to see the next place.
It certainly couldn't hurt
to look at other options I'd set up for the day,
but I had a feeling about this home.

Home.

Besides...I liked the carpet.

Daily Decision

If I open the front curtains,
the neighbors think I'm available for constructive criticism.
The doorbell doesn't work, so,
the elderly lady who survived The Red Army
        bangs on my front window
The pounding startles me with its suddenness,
but if I don't answer, she comes back
Repeatedly banging on the glass with her fist
I can't ignore her
She's amassed decades of sorrow in her life
She's lost so many friends at her age
She needs someone to talk to

If I open the front curtains,
the woman who uses her husband's marijuana
        shakes the screen door
The rattling startles me with its suddenness,
but if I don't answer, she calls out my name
as she walks the perimeter, shouting at each window
I can't ignore her
She has so many problems with her husband
And her daughter, her mother, her son,
her ex-husband, and so on

If I open the curtains,
the fellow from a few streets over stops by
to update me on his political campaign.

If I open the curtains,
the postman stops to ask directions to deliver packages
to some address he doesn't recognize.

If I open the curtains,
a random stranger wants to know if I own a cat
which might be responsible for the dead lizard on the sidewalk.

If I open the curtains,
the lawn care people want to make sure I wasn't mad
when I cancelled my service
or when I told them to stop calling
or when I told them to stop stopping by.

If I open the curtains,
the bright
and beautiful
Florida sunshine
streams in on beams of freshness.

I make the decision to pull the cord
and the light slides in,
chasing anxiety somewhere I can't see it
and filling up all of the room
except for a shadow,
a silhouette on the floor
of a neighbor
peering in the window,
waiting for me to open the curtains.

There's a Gnat in My Coffee

One of those empowerment-coach, guru types
gave a TED-like talk with a lapel mic,
      coating his words with instant credibility,
      so that they dripped with wisdom
      upon multiple generations who were dragged
      to the audience.
(Some of us against our will.)
And he quothe unto the masses:
"The key to joyous prosperity
in your spiritual awakening
is to embrace the small stuff
while visualizing and speaking
to the universe the bigger picture
of what you want out of life
with a positive, optimistic worldview of self."

Rather than let him analyze my handwriting
for symptoms of pessimism and sociopathy,
I returned to my reality of the 12% tax bracket
(or whatever it is this month)
where Monday brings the small pleasure of hot coffee
(with pumpkin spice creamer).

As I stare into my cup of positive, optimistic worldview,
contemplating my joyous prosperity
versus sleep-deprived data entry,
I see a dark speck floating on the surface.

There's a gnat in my coffee.

I question his spiritual awakening.
Did it peak before his end?
Did this creature sweat his cares away
      in a caffeinated sauna of positive optimism?

With a sigh for the tiny life snuffed out,
I use the dry tip of my finger
      to lift his body from the meniscus...
      ...and wipe him on my jeans.

Maybe the TED-talk guru was right.
I embrace the fact that today,
I'm not the gnat.

Imitation

After hours of the dog's incessant barking
A neighbor steps to his back porch
To scream at the poor thing
I'm not sure hound dogs understand
Streams of obscenities
But they certainly interpret an angry tone
As do the neighborhood corvids
The dog silenced, slinks under a patio chair
Gives way to a dark feathered soldier
Who lands above his wicker shelter
With a tilt of sun-glistening head,
The raven considers the scene
And lets forth his own stream of obscenities
Barking incessantly at the neighbor

I Scoff at Anger Management

Call it rebellion, depression, rage...
I don't think acrimony has a singular label
when it's constant
and surging
frothing under spray against a jagged cliff wall
where I bang my fist for emphasis
during a team-building retreat.
There is power in a man's
Creepy-eyed, red-faced anger
which can be harnessed for action
or suppressed
depending on one's goals
one's stability,
unlike the stupidity
of a driver who's been cut off
or the online troll
whose lack of logic's been ignored
or the child without discipline
screaming to have his way.
Mere amateurs, I say.
All of them!
True, real-life, furious exasperation
takes years of corporate management to attain.

Waiting for an Audience

It's no good daydreaming out the corner window
when he knows his time is wasted here.
Wasted while he wonders when his greatness will be discovered,
when Corporate America will turn its collective head
in unabashed awe...

and gasp.

God, but promotions are a long time in coming.
And raises even longer.
Praises are few and far between,
when he's stuck on the boss's flypaper
shaped like a mobius strip
waving in front of a pedestal fan
in an office with a broken grandfather clock
where the pendulum of his career is forever lodged
in the abyss of the fulcrum's swing...

waiting.

He waits for recognition that never comes,
until he's caught staring out the boss's window.

Turtle Lights

Over a hundred souls dropped into the sand
Over sixty nights ago
And slept nestled in partial security

Last night, as the sun dropped burnt-orange into the ocean
The souls percolated
From their burial in a worry of life

In the space between the eruption and the surf
Where the scramble
And the dash meld into a frenetic rush

A bright night beach teemed with death
And disorientation
As nature fed upon its most confused

Of the hundred and twelve who climbed
Out of the nest
I found one on the court across the highway

Weakened, dry, but whole
He has a chance at life
If we can get him to water and shade

His hundred and eleven siblings
Eaten by shorebirds, crabs, tires,
And racoons that hunt by the condo lights

Cancer Doesn't Scare Me

Call it ennui
or faith in my Great Physician,
but I didn't fear death
coming for me.

I felt its hand
once or twice while hospitalized
for procedures' problems.
Looked in his eyes,

looked in his face,
and merely waited for the scythe
that never struck me down.
Not all the way.

And I wonder now,
Does death wait in the shadows
for apathy to subside
before appearing

to me again?
It's a lie to say I beat cancer
when I didn't fight.
I merely didn't die.

Surprisingly,
I moved through the experience twice,
watching needles and tubes
deliver meds,

fluids, and poisons.
The scars remain all over my body,
as if I have a right
to show them off,

when all I did
was stare down the specter of death,
as if daring him to reach in,
and let me go.

Tears at a Murderer's Grave

They covered up the sun today,
as you requested
But it's taking longer to drain the oceans than they expected
So, the end of the world has to wait for tomorrow
Possibly Thursday
I feel as if you can tell it causes me anxiety
That even now, you have your finger on the pulse of my soul
Ah, we had something dangerous the first time I felt that touch,
And your sly smile said you knew it
Like the promise in an egg's first trembling
But you never know what will come of it
Until the darn thing hatches
Like all the henchmen before you
You were one psychological drama after another
Right up to the end of the world
And when you left
My heart broke with relief

Simple Requests

I don't care what meals you bring me
  Just as long as you're liberal with the butter
  And frosting
  And serve the chocolate cake fresh from the fridge

I don't care if my crayons are sharp
  Just as long as I have plenty
  And paper
  And coloring books with bunnies and turtles

I don't care what ward you put me in
  Just as long as I have peace
  And calm
  And sunshine streaming through the window

Spots

At one end of the light fixture
Two dark dots
Sit amid a blob
Of what looks like a splot
Of rusty water drop
Making me wonder
About electrical current
And flow
And fire hazards
It makes me wonder what
Could get inside the light
And splatter
In that manner
Oozing goo into a spot
That looks like rusted rot

Tiny Reflections of God

They're all out of place
This man a veteran of wars past
Fought to defend someone's rights
Other than his own, it would seem
And now he lies against a stucco building
Without guttering
Using a burnt cookie sheet
Scarred by its former owner's neglect
To shield his face from the downpour
Of South Florida's latest storm
A rain band passing through
And the Bell's Vireo with his quieted warbling
Who hops to the sheet as if expecting an answer
When he taps his insect-structured beak
One inch of query tapping, rapping politely
A black eye peeking from a bulbous body
This man a veteran of wars past
Lifts the shelter slightly
And the diminutive bird flits under
Out of the onslaught

How Far the Prize

She once saw a goal unreachable
Well-meaning adults warned looking away from it
Someone suggested starting with One Step toward it
One crevice, one hill, one outcropping at a time
Each day moving forward,
Alternately fording streams
And scuffing her knuckles and knees on rocky walls
Brought her to a valley
From which she could look up
Look back at momentous struggles
Times when moving forward
Was arduous beyond endurance
Yet what beauty in the landscape she beheld
In the trials she'd met with crimson or fiery orange-sunset success.
Roaring waters' distant thundering demanded a decision
You can't sit in the valley without consequence
Even inaction has ramification
One step at a time may take longer than desired
Each crevice may be surmountable
How far ahead does one look to see the prize
Without overwhelming the soul with the
Length, width, slope of the road?
How far back does one look for inspiration
Without longing for a return to the comfortable known?
How long can one stand in indecision before momentum is lost?
Kinetic energy building with the rush of water moving
She grasps the rocks protruding from the cliff wall
And begins the next day's climb
Forward
Toward the goal reachable

Try Tomorrow

I get there are days when it's tough
Life's got this way of mixing up stuff
Medication, vacation, or pure relaxation
Don't always bring about justification
To think getting up is enough

Sometimes it's not easy to survive
Maybe even harder to thrive
Look at your track record so far
Look in the mirror at the shiner you are
Each day is one more succeeding to strive

With one step in front of the other
Climb one hill after another
Turns into a mountain you've crossed
A summit you've won and not lost
Triumphs in whatever weather

Make me this promise, my friend
Take this permission at day's end
For a cry before going to bed
When tomorrow comes up be ready to hit it
With a smile at your toughness instead

Time and Space

When did you last lift your lashes
sodden as they may have been
When did you last raise your gaze
expecting to see beauty in the mirror?
Don't you know you'll see kindness
looking back from behind your eyes
And wisdom formed within wrinkles
that curve from life, reality, love

When did you last grant permission
to sit quietly on a plush cushion
To feel softness that permeates stillness
and deep evenings of starring Heavens

Your entire being knows how to embrace
The gentleness of yourself,
Your entire self knows how to get back
To steeped in the peacefullest moments of you

We're all on this rock together, yet
Using different spaceships for random orbit
If your suit's sprung a leak lately,
I've got a spare can of sealant spray.
Maybe that fix isn't permanent,
Not all repairs carry you all the way
Some are just meant to get you to the next station
Some patches merely remind you
To take time to see the beautiful person I see
In the reflections off panels in space

About the Author

Sandy Lender is a magazine editor by day and author of girl-power fantasy novels by night. You can check out her **author page on Amazon** or follow her facebook page at Fantasy Author Sandy Lender. She lives in Florida where she volunteers in sea turtle conservation and parrot rescue. She has two APEX Awards in technical writing and a 2019 IMADJINN Award for Best Literary Fiction Novel.

Other Works by Sandy Lender

Choices Meant for Gods
Choices Meant for Kings
Choices Meant for All
What Choices We Made, Vol I
What Choices We Made, Vol II
Problems on Eldora Prime
Problems above Pangaea Moon
Problems in Annady's Core
May Your Heart Be Light
We Can't Let You In, A Diary of the PyreDees Plague of 2016
She's Not Broken, IMADJINN 2019 Best Literary Fiction Novel
How to Train Your Human: A Guide for Parrots
Move the Stars: A Gentle Dragons Novel

"A Legacy Protected," *Winter's Night, Vol I*
"Desecrated Ring," Keith Publications Halloween
"Dragons in Crisis," *Winter's Night, Vol II*
"Perceptions on New Year's Eve," *A Yuletide Wish* Anthology
"Woman off the Grid," *Wild Women* Anthology
"Della Finds Her Gift," TulipTree *Genre* Anthology

Visit **www.SandyLenderInk.com**
Poems of Trials, Triumphs, and Turtles
First edition copyright 2020

www.ingramcontent.com/pod-product-compliance
Lightning Source LLC
Chambersburg PA
CBHW020443030426
42337CB00014B/1376